Time Heals All Things

by Molly Hazelwood

CHAPTERS

chapter one

sunlight

5

we may not see
in our times of pain
that we will
one day be healed
but we will
it is a law of nature

-time heals all things

blessed is the light
that beams from our sun
and feeds life on earth
and connects living things

-sunlight

there is nothing we can do
quite as sweet
as love one another

-circulate

we need only look
at the magnificence
of our planet
to see the shining light
of a creator's joy

-creator

the world would be
so much simpler
if we all just
said what we think
instead of hiding it

-truth

some people
simply must
be let go of

-let go

you don't need
anyone or anything
to be who you're
meant to be

-meant to be

self-love
is a never-ending battle
it is a journey
rather than a destination
a journey of a thousand miles
taken step by step

but do not worry
you will get there.

-self-love

our society teaches us
that our value
is determined
by status and money
but that just isn't true

-*you are so much more*

the strongest thing
someone can do
is forgive someone
who doesn't deserve it

-forgiveness

she was the sun
hidden
behind the clouds
waiting
for her time to shine

-waiting

if you never put yourself
in new situations
if you're never
uncomfortable
or learning something new
you're wasting your life

-waste

the moonlight shows
through the windows
and i lay here
in my bed
alone

missing you
wishing on the stars
that our paths
would cross
again

-wishing on moonlight pt. ii

selfish people
do not deserve
your energy

-learn to be selfish sometimes

worry
solves nothing
and helps no one

so quiet your soul
as best you can

-worry

continue to suffer
by staying in the same place
or suffer
the pain
of allowing change to happen
it's your choice

-don't be afraid to change

when you feel
most helpless
is when you are
closest
to breaking through

-breakthrough

never make decisions
based on what others think
you are the only one
who can light your path
to true happiness

-light your path

your past
made you
who you are
today

but don't let that
be an excuse
not to move on
and grow
towards happiness

life goes on
even if it feels
like it never will

-life goes on

do not be sad
because you
don't have
someone else's life

spend time
improving your life
rather than coveting others'

-life

things
will always
get better

-i promise

i hope one day
you wake up
in the middle of the night
next to your husband or wife
and thank your lucky stars
knowing
that you got
everything you wanted
in life

-my wish for you pt. ii

you owe it to yourself
to do everything
you possibly can
to make your dreams
come true

-dreams

do not waste your time
trying to change
how others see you

let your light
speak for itself

-speak

be careful
who you
surround yourself with

negative people
can suck the life
out of your dreams
before you've even started

-be careful

everything
will be okay

do not lose sight
of that fact

even if you can't see it
right now
the sun will always rise

-the sun always rises

chapter two

soil

where you are in life
is only a starting place
it is not
a prison sentence

-build your own future

beware of people
who are willing
to take
everything you give
and give nothing
in return

-reciprocity

hold on to your faith
things will work out.

-faith

do not allow others
to discourage you
from getting what you want
in life

you have only one life
do not waste it
making others feel better
by putting yourself down

-stand up

broken people
love the deepest

-deep

when your problems
seem bigger than ever before
look inside yourself
and take heart
for your willpower
to get through this
is bigger
than anything
life could ever
throw at you

-will

do not waste the present
on the concerns of the past

-live now

only give yourself completely
to people
who give as much to you
as you give to them

-back and forth

nothing will ever be
as sweet
as your "i love you's"

-*love*

your life
should be a testament
to what you are

-testament

sadness
only makes
happiness
all the sweeter

-relativity

i will never get you back
and for the first time
in a long time
i am okay with that.

-get you back

as long as you have
hope in your heart

you are immortal.

-hope

living a good life
and treating others well
is its own reward

-*treat others well*

forgive others
even
when they don't
deserve it

-forgive

you have the power
to change who you are

-never forget that

49

today
is a brand new
beginning.

seize it
and change your life

this is the sign
you've been waiting for

-*sign*

we were not born
for cubicles

we are not hamsters
in a cage

-freedom

true power
is taking responsibility
for your problems
and face them
without excuses

-without excuses

all these
beautiful people

artificially
divided.

-divided

you said
you never loved me

nothing hurt
quite as much
as that

-pain

you will get
what you deserve
that's the law of karma

your responsibility
is simply to make your fate
a good one

-karma

i miss
everything about
what we used to be

-us

your hands
could warm
the coldest heart

-*your hands*

you don't know pain
until you've been separated
from a person
who feels like
the other half of you

-*pain*

chapter three

light

61

healing
takes time

its hard to accept that
and even harder
to wait through it

-patience

if a man
is afraid
of your power

dump him

you are too good
for someone
who is afraid
to play with fire

-play with fire

you have to love yourself
before
you can love
anyone else

-else

nothing
has ever tasted
quite as sweet
as the taste
of your lips
on my lips
that very first time

-kissing in the rain

nothing
has ever felt
simultaneously
so amazing
and so painful
as loving you
and losing you

-love & loss

acknowledge your pain.

that
is the first step
towards healing.

-acknowledge your pain

you have
so much
more potential
than you know.

you
are a seed
just waiting
to bloom
into a beautiful flower

-bloom

if losing them
didn't hurt

you never
really loved them

-hurt

do not be afraid to lose
things.

it is only through
acceptance of loss
that we can be truly free.

-truly free

your life will not always be
as hard as it is now.

there is no river so long
that it doesn't contain a bend.

-*the river will always bend*

don't fall in love
with people
who are still in love
with someone else

all they're doing
is looking
for pieces of who they want
in you

-they don't care about you
pt.ii

be careful of people
who disrespect those
who are beneath them.

their true feelings are
revealed
when they are tested
in this way.

-beneath

your smile
is far more beautiful
than any sunrise
could ever be

-your smile

when you are feeling down
take time
to look at your life
and the ways
it is good

do not concentrate
too harshly
on the bad

-contrast

let the light
into your life
and into your heart

-the light

never forget those
who have left
a positive impact
on your life

-never forget

a rose
is just as beautiful
if it bloomed
in royal gardens
or in the dirt
of a poor country

and so are you.

-*you are beautiful*

remember to give yourself
some credit
for everything
you have already
accomplished

-credit

one cannot be
truly happy
without giving to others.

-*giving*

pursue all the things
you know in your heart
you are meant to be

-pursuit

life does not close a door
without opening a new one

-doors

you reap what you sow

so remember to
sow good things.

-sow

do not be afraid
to express yourself
and be everything
you know you can be

-express

nothing has ever
hurt me
or pleased me
as much as your love

-romance & heartbreak

chapter four

life

being broke
doesn't mean
having no money

it means
you have no more dreams
left to dream

-broke

how do you expect
the universe
to put good things
in your life
when you constantly
speak negativity
into your life?

-negativity

there is nothing quite as toxic
to one's soul
as not forgiving
someone else

-toxic

the only people
worthy of staying
in your life

are those
who work hard
to keep you
in theirs.

-worth it

always be true
to your roots.

they will keep you
in place
even when the mightiest
winds
how fiercely.

-roots

it is okay
to admit
you don't understand.

only then
can you learn.

-learn

sex
is not a dirty thing

and it should be enjoyed
by anyone
who wants to
without repercussions

-*sex*

there is nothing
quite as beautiful
as two people
falling in love
drawing closer
as snowflakes fall
keeping each other warm
against the coldest night

-love versus the coldest night
pt. ii

take heart;
the best things
are still
yet to come.

-take heart

only through faith
in yourself
can you move forward.

-move forward

take your revenge
by loving people
rather than hurting them.

-revenge

don't expect
yourself
to be perfect.

no one ever has been
and no one ever will be.

-perfect

there is no better self-care
than cutting off people
who are toxic for you.

-self-care

don't give second chances
to those
who only realized your worth
by losing you

they never appreciated it
in the first place

-second chances

do not pretend
to be anyone
you are not

you are beautiful
just as you are.

-be yourself

in order to love
someone else

you must first
understand
who you are.

-self

life is too short
to be with people
who don't make you
happy.

-life is short

the world doesn't know
who you truly are

so do not take their insults
to heart

they know not
what they say.

-insults

the scariest realization
is how easy it is
to leave
and how much power
you have
when you do it.

-leave

be careful who
you open up to.

some people
use your vulnerability
as a weapon.

-trust carefully

when someone hurts you
they don't get
to say
that they didn't

*-they can't take away
the truth*

just because
someone
hurt you
once before

doesn't mean

that everyone
who comes after
will do the same thing.

-hurt

heartbreak is inevitable.

the only thing we can do
is love those
who would let us down
gently.

-gently

you were
thirsty
for love

and i
was a tsunami

we were destined
to end
in destruction.

-tsunami

CPSIA information can be obtained
at www.ICGtesting.com
Printed in the USA
BVOW07s0057230218
508940BV00024B/168/P